YOUR MONEY

SAVING MY MONEY

Claire Llewellyn

illustrated by Mike Gordon

WINDMILL
BOOKS

Published in 2017 by **Windmill Books**,
an Imprint of Rosen Publishing
29 East 21st Street, New York, NY 10010

Text copyright © Claire Llewellyn
Illustrations copyright © Mike Gordon
Senior editor: Camilla Lloyd
Designer: Paul Cherrill
Digital Color: Carl Gordon

Cataloging-in-Publication Data
Names: Llewellyn, Claire.
Title: Saving my money / Claire Llewellyn and Mike Gordon.
Description: New York : Windmill Books, 2017 | Series: Your money | Includes index.
Identifiers: ISBN 9781499481945 (pbk.) | ISBN 9781499481952 (library bound) |
    ISBN 9781508193098 (6 pack)
Subjects: LCSH: Saving and investment--Juvenile literature. | Children--Finance,
    Personal--Juvenile literature.
Classification: LCC HB822.L56 2017 | DDC 332.024--dc23

Manufactured in the United States of America
CPSIA Compliance Information: Batch #BW17PK: For Further Information contact
Rosen Publishing, New York, New York at 1-800-237-9932.

SAVING
MY MONEY

Written by
Claire Llewellyn

Illustrated by
Mike Gordon

WINDMILL
BOOKS

Have you ever seen something you really
want but don't have the money to buy?

You could ask Mom or Dad for it ...

Saving means putting money aside
so that you can use it in the future.

If you save money steadily, then your savings
will grow and grow – just like tiny seeds.

So how do you start saving money?

Every time you get some money, don't spend all of it ...

8

... put half of it in your money box
and keep it somewhere safe.

Saving can be tricky at times.
It's very tempting to spend your money...

... and there are so many fun things to buy.

But if you keep saving, not spending, your money,
then week by week, your savings will grow.

Before you know it, you'll reach your goal ...

13

... to pay for things that cost a lot.

15

When you are saving a lot of money,
it's best to have a savings account in a bank.

Your money will earn interest. This means that a little extra money is added to your savings, helping them to grow even more!

In the future, you can use your savings
to buy something extra special ...

... or do something you really want to do.

Saving money is a good habit.
What would you like to do in the future?

What could you save for?

Notes for Parents and Teachers

We all need to be able to manage our money and make financial decisions. The four books in the *Your Money* series are intended as a first step along this path. Based on children's everyday lives, the series is a lighthearted introduction to money, everyday financial transactions, planning and saving and financial choices.

Saving my Money explains how, by spending sensibly, children can save some of their money. It discusses how saving helps us to plan for the future and enables us to buy or do the things we want. It looks at the best places to save money and introduces the concept of earning interest in a savings account.

Suggested follow-up activities

• Devise a game with children to be played with dice. Think of examples of getting money, spending money and saving money. For example, "You get your pocket money today, move forward 2 squares;" or "You lose 50¢. Move back 3 squares."

• Make a collection of different types of money boxes. Which one does the job best? Why? Which one is the children's favorite? Why? Now ask the children to design a money box of their own. Make sure it's easier to put money in than take it out!

• Imagine you are going to buy a pet. Come up with a list of questions you would have to ask.

For example, what would the pet cost to buy? What essential equipment would the pet need? What other costs might be necessary? Then take the children to a pet shop and find the answers to your questions.

• Take children inside a bank so that they can see what happens there. You could suggest they open a savings account and save some of their money.

• Ask children to think of one thing they would really like to buy and one thing they would really like to do. Help them to find out how much it would cost. If they saved $1 a week, how long would they take to buy it? Can they think of any ways they could get or earn the money?

• What things do adults need to save for? What are the most expensive things that they are likely to need or want? Ask children for suggestions or give them picture clues.

• Get children to draw a picture of something they dream of doing in the future. Get them to write a caption – for example, "One day, I want to ride a camel in the desert."

BOOKS TO READ

Learning About Money: Saving Money by Mary Firestone
(First Fact Books, 2004)

Using Money by Rebecca Rissman
(Heinemann Library, 2010)

WEBSITES

For web resources related to the subject of this book, go to:
www.windmillbooks.com/weblinks and select this book's title.

INDEX